T0358074

SPITFIRE
War Heroes of the Sky

R.T. Watts

KNOWLEDGE
BOOKS AND SOFTWARE

7

Teacher Notes:

This is the true story of Johan Anton 'Tony' Stroeve, a Dutch adolescent who made a daring escape from the German Gestapo to Britain where he became a fighter pilot for the RAF during WW2. This story provides opportunities for students to explore the attributes of courage, determination and resilience and touches on the atrocities of the German army under the dictatorship of Hitler during WW2. After the war, Tony Stroeve lived the rest of his life in Australia. Tony applied to fly again in Australia but ironically, he failed the eyesight test.

Discussion points for consideration:

1. Why did Tony decide to escape from Holland? Why did his first attempt fail?

2. Find examples in the story where Tony and his comrades showed incredible bravery and mateship.

3. Share your opinions on Germany's actions during WW2.

4. Germany was eventually defeated, but at what cost? Discuss the impact of the war on both sides.

Sight words, difficult to decode words, and infrequent words to be introduced and practised before reading this book:

Silesia, occupied, Jewish, Indonesia, Hurricane, Gestapo, together, engineers, weighed, equipment, thousands, brought, different, pinpoint, honour, funerals, Commonwealth, underneath, buildings, radioed, concentration, dangerous, controlled, continued.

Contents

1. About World War 2

World War 2 started in 1939 when Germany attacked Poland. Germany, under Adolf Hitler, was gaining power. Poland had a dispute with Germany over an area called Silesia. Germany fought the Polish army and won.

England and France had a deal with Poland to make sure they would help each other. The deal was to go to war if any one of the countries was attacked by Germany. France and Britain declared war on Germany but did nothing to help Poland.

Germany attacked France, Belgium and Holland. Holland said it was not taking sides, but Germany still took control. Germany then started bombing Britain.

3

2. Holland is Occupied

Holland was taken over by Germany. The Dutch people were now occupied by Germany. This meant that all rules and ways of doing things were done by Germany.

The Jewish people were the first to know about the Nazis. All Jewish people had to wear an ID. This was a yellow Star of David.

Schools were told that all Jewish children and teachers must wear the yellow star. At one school the next day after the new rule, **all** of the teachers turned up with a yellow star on their clothes. This was to show unity with the Jewish children and teachers.

3. Escape Plan Number 1

Tony Stroeve was a teenager in Holland when Germany took over. His family were against Germany.

Tony's brother Jan was a pilot for the Dutch airline KLM. Jan left his plane in Indonesia. He would not fly it back to Holland. The German secret police (Gestapo) was looking for Tony's brother. But Jan was in Britain now, still flying KLM planes.

Tony wanted to escape German control. He talked to some of his friends about going to Britain. They had to be very careful. The Gestapo would kill them. They met some people who could help them escape by train to Spain and then to Britain.

Tony and his friends decided to escape. They would get their stuff and meet at the train station. Another mate turned up and told him it was a trap. He warned his friends, but they went anyway. They were never heard of again. The Gestapo had caught them, and they were shot.

The Nazis were now taking control of Holland. The Jewish people were told they would be sent to work camps. They were told to leave their houses. Some hid like Anne Frank, some escaped to Britain, and others were taken by the Nazis.

In 1941, there were 154,887 Dutch Jews, and after the war, there were only 14,346 Jews left in Holland. Most of the missing Jews had been murdered in concentration camps.

4. Escape Plan Number 2

Tony did not want to hang around any longer. Tony wanted to fight this evil force. He escaped on a boat to Britain. The Gestapo came to his mother and told her he had been shot and killed at sea.

When he got to Britain, he told them he wanted to join the air force. First thing was to make sure he was not a spy. He then went and had all the tests and checked to see if he could join the air force.

5. Training on Spitfires

His first choice was to become a
fighter pilot. If this was not possible,
he would be a bomber pilot. Bomber
pilots have a higher chance of dying.

After passing all the tests, Tony started
on pilot training. He flew a small plane
called a Tiger Moth. His teacher sat in
the back and made sure he did
everything correctly. After that he went
to Canada to train to be a fighter pilot.
It was here he met his favourite fighter
plane: the Spitfire.

The Spitfire was Britain's fighter plane.
These planes only held a single
person, and they were very fast. They
had four machine guns and were able
to fight any of Germany's planes. They
had a Rolls Royce engine which was
like the engine from a souped-up
sports car. It could fly very fast when
you needed to escape from a German
fighter. The other great British fighter
plane was the Hurricane.

All the training took place in Canada. It was fun but dangerous. Tony was learning to fly low to the ground to escape German radar. This low flying was very dangerous, and one of the team was killed when they hit the ground. Another pilot was killed doing a roll to avoid an attack plane. There were now only 8 of the 10 who started training. Tony got his flight wings and was sent back to Britain. More training continued and he joined a fighting unit. He was now ready to start the battle.

17

6. Fighting at Last

In the morning, the pilots had a coffee and some doughnuts. They put on their flight gear and made sure they were ready for the freezing cold. They then had to wait for a call to run to the Spitfires.

They had about 90 minutes of flying time, or about 350 litres of fuel. The fuel was used up at 5 litres per minute so you could not stay up too long.

The bombers flew a long distance to Berlin and back. Tony's team was sent up to protect the planes on their way back. The German ME and FU fighters were attacking the bombers. On his first day, Tony was called to fly up and protect the bombers returning from Germany.

I opened fire at one of them and saw a few hits on his cowling, but he put his stick down and went below me. I turned sharply and tried to get on his tail and when I almost got on his tail a Hurricane whooshed past and gave the German a few seconds' blast that blew off his tail and sent him down like a ton of bricks. While this was happening another FW got in my sight and flew right across, getting on to the tail of a B-19. I turned and was on his back before he knew it, gave him a burst and saw my spurt hitting his wings and canopy which flew off and almost hit me. The FW went straight up in the air and I saw the pilot jumping out, but had no time to see if his chute opened as I had to watch out not to be jumped on by another Jerry.

7. Attacking Planes

The team's next call was even more serious. A bomber group was under attack again. The team flew up to meet the bombers and attack the German fighter planes. The bomber group was flying back from a bombing mission attacking Berlin.

Tony flew down and machine-gunned a ME plane. On the way to the attack, another ME saw him and went after him. He was told by one of the team he was being followed. He peeled off to the side to make a loop to try and get behind the enemy, but lost sight of the ME. The team shot down 2 enemy planes that day without losing any themselves.

The radar along the coast of Britain picked up a massive attack of bombers. This time over 100 German bombers were heading towards them. They had to go up and give the Germans a big welcome!

This time they were diving down towards the planes and trying to shoot their four engines. Once their engines were not working, the bombers would crash.

They had to make sure they were close before they fired their machine guns. The guns fire bullets the same size as a .303 rifle. The machine guns could shoot very fast.

23

They flew back over France to England and landed safely. The cafe, or mess, was always open now. The pilots could go and eat when they got a chance.

The pilots went to the mess to eat, but most just sat there a lot of the time. They did not say much, but some could not stop their hands shaking. There was no time to think of your missing mate or the danger. You had to rest and report back that afternoon, ready to go up again. There was no time to talk or give high-fives, you just had to try and deal with the horror of war.

8. Rescue

A battle over Holland was taking place. Tony was attacking some German ME fighters when he was attacked. The underneath of his plane was hit. Bullets shot through the cabin. One bullet hit the steering gear.

Tony could no longer steer the Spitfire properly. He broke off and headed towards Britain again. He was joined by some of the team. They stayed with him as his plane was smashed with bullets.

The Spitfire was losing height and was about to crash. He radioed that he was heading into the sea off Britain. He crashed the plane into the sea. His mates stayed above in a circle for a little while.

Many aircrews were being killed. When your mate did not return, you were told he was missing. You did not know for sure, but most were killed.

There were many funerals. The aircrew was given the notice to get into their best uniform and wait. Everyone would be picked up in a bus. The bus would drive to the church for the service. The aircrew would be the line of honour. The coffin would be carried into and out of the church.

After the service, there was tea and cakes. And then it was back to the airbase. Britain lost over 60,000 RAF people.

If the aircrew died over Germany, they were buried properly.

9. Looking for the V1 and V2

German rocket engineers were way ahead of Britain, Russia and the USA. They built new rockets called the V1 and then the V2. They were made to carry a bomb which weighed a tonne. It had rocket fuel and a setting so that it flew directly to the target.

Germany sent over 1000 of these rockets towards Britain. The V1 and V2 rockets killed thousands of British people. Hitler thought it would scare the British so much that they would give up. This did not happen.

The rockets were not able to hit a moving target or hit a ship, or aircraft. It was a great rocket but was not going to change the war for Germany.

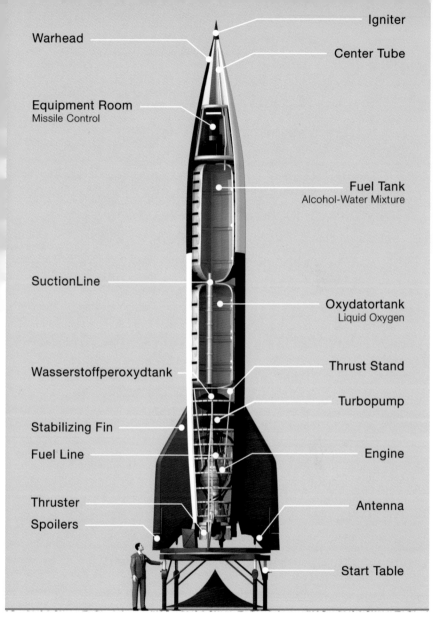

Igniter

Warhead

Center Tube

Equipment Room
Missile Control

Fuel Tank
Alcohol-Water Mixture

SuctionLine

Oxydatortank
Liquid Oxygen

Wasserstoffperoxydtank

Thrust Stand

Turbopump

Stabilizing Fin

Fuel Line

Engine

Thruster

Antenna

Spoilers

Start Table

31

Meeting up with his brother Jan was always special for Tony. Jan lived in Bristol and Tony could get there by bus. They would spend the weekend together.

They could only spend a short time together, as Jan was flying planes to other parts of Europe and America. Tony had to go back to the airbase as he only had 24-hour leave.

The city offered cafes, eating places and movie places. There was plenty to see and do. It was a good weekend away from the airbase.

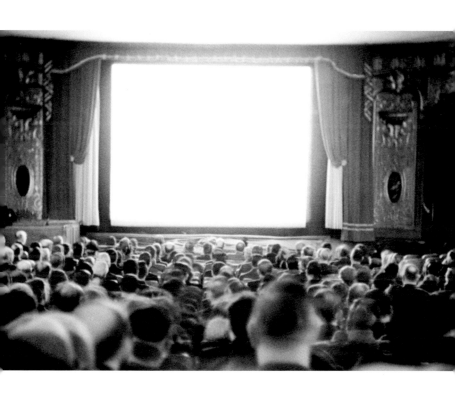

Food was always good for the pilots. However, food in Britain and Australia during the war was short. All the food went to soldiers and aircrew.

People had very limited food. You were given a ration card. This ration card meant you could get a certain number of eggs, bacon, milk and meat. The ration cards were for many things. It meant every person got what they needed to survive.

Tony was lucky as he could also get food and things from his brother. His brother was a pilot who travelled all over the world. Jan brought back a lot of different foods, such as bananas and oranges.

35

Britain and Germany were at war. Australia, New Zealand, Canada and other Commonwealth countries joined Britain to help them win.

The United States of America was sending equipment. The American people had no interest in going to war. This view was changing slowly.

Germany tried to make sure that the USA would stay out of the war. The USA decided only to send equipment and not go to war against Germany. The USA changed to help Britain with soldiers too. This was when Germany knew they would lose.

Tony was flying low, as usual, to be under the radar and stay hidden. He saw a series of buildings and barbed wire fences. As he flew past, he turned to see what it was, and again flew low over the top. He looked down and saw people inside the concentration camp. Tony turned the Spitfire back and headed low directly towards the watchtower. He saw flashes of fire coming at him, and he waited until he was right on them, and then fired his machine guns.

This was one of the many concentration camps set up in German-controlled countries. These were holding camps for the Jewish people and others, before most were killed. More than 6 million people were killed in concentration camps.

10. D-Day "Operation Overlord"

Germany was under attack from Russia. In Italy, Britain and its allies were fighting German forces. The next stage was a direct ground attack into France. This was called *D-Day* which happened in June, 1944. There were more than 350,000 soldiers landing in France.

Tony's job was to help on D-Day. His group had to fly low and attack any enemy position that they could find. He shot at trains, trucks, guns, and planes.

He had 90 minutes in the air and then had to get ammo and fuel. On D-Day, he did 4 missions over France which was over 9 hours in the air. This was a big day of over 16 hours.

D-Day It's On!

Tuesday, 6th of June, the whole station was in a panic. We were chased out of bed and breakfast was put on at five for the entire base. All planes were to be made ready for scrambles as from now. Pilots were to be ready fully combat dressed and the spare kit ready, packed for transfer at short notice. This certainly meant that the big show was on. All over the base you could hear the Spits' engines being warmed up and tested.

Tony was one of the lucky ones to stay alive. Half of all the air crews were killed. These air crews were young men who left their homes to go to war. This was a terrible war where both sides bombed each other's cities. German cities were smashed, and little of the old places were left. Hannover had no buildings still standing. A lot of people died in Germany and Britain from the bombings.

After the war Tony and his family, moved to Australia where he lived until his death in 2000.

The Few

"Never in the field of human conflict have so much been owed to so few."

Winston Churchill, August, 1940

Johan Anton 'Tony' Stroeve
Born: 2nd September, 1921 Died: 9th June, 2000

Word Bank

together	engineers
weighed	equipment
thousands	brought
target	different
pinpoint	limited
honour	brother
funerals	weekend
Commonwealth	underneath
buildings	smashed
standing	radioed
terrible	crashed
concentration	dangerous
controlled	continued